MW01529225

EGO &
EMPATHY

Let's Crush!

EGO & EMPATHY

**A 3-STEP GUIDE TO INFLUENCING YOURSELF
AND THE WORLD AROUND YOU**

Mike Cooper

© 2017 Mike Cooper
All rights reserved.

ISBN: 154550217X
ISBN 13: 9781545502174
Library of Congress Control Number: 2017907813
CreateSpace Independent Publishing Platform
North Charleston, South Carolina

CONTENTS

ABOUT THIS BOOK

This book was written as a guide in a world of uncertainty and confusion.

It presents a clear and effective step by step process, describing how it is possible to successfully influence yourself and the world around you.

In this book the powerful tools, strategies and techniques that have been handed down through generations to those willing to learn, can be found. The author takes no credit for these ideas and is simply a student, himself, in the game of life, sharing his own experiences to offer a perspective that was sometimes learned the hard way.

If you are a leader, a parent, a teacher, an influencer or a persuader of any sort this book will be of value. The principles within are relevant to us all.

The pages contain a combination of real life examples, stories and experiences all wrapped up in a package that will resonate with any reader seeking ways to enhance an ability to be productively influential.

Let me be very clear. This is not a "How to get Rich" book. This book is about learning to influence and successfully persuade. It's a 3-Step personal guide that simplifies the art of successful influence and persuasion.

The chapters offer a step by step analysis of the challenges to be expected when selling and persuading, and how to sell with certainty, and by design, rather than simply by chance.

FOREWORD

I have a clear memory of being 16 years old and asking strangers for change at a bus station in Peterborough Ontario.

Uncertain where I was going to sleep that night, I felt scared, alone and angry. Thankfully, owing to the kindness of friends and non-family members, my first experience of being without a home didn't last longer than 2 weeks. By the time I was 17, however, I had lived with 6 different families and attended 7 different schools. It was a lot of change in a short amount of time.

There was a point in my life when I would blame others for my misfortunes. Now I no longer blame anyone for the paths I chose. I know that my misfortunes have always has been the result of the choices I made. Actions have reactions and I was just unaware what the negative consequences could be.

The adults in my life did the best they could with an intense little dude like me. I challenged authority, craved attention and had no regard for other people's feelings. There was no real option left but to let me figure it out in my way.

With no consistency or stability in my life, I inherited and developed some interesting patterns. Stuck in a vortex of my own self-sabotage, time continued to go by and my choices were not improving. Piling on the layers of self-imposed pain and suffering, I seemed to learn most things the hard way… if I even learned them at all.

By age 31, I had been arrested 9 times and severely struggled with many forms of addiction. One of those arrests was when I crashed my truck while heavily intoxicated. I had no license, no money and no credit. It is safe to say that I do know what it feels like to make "questionable choices".

I discovered hitchhiking at age 12 because there was no vehicle in our household. I can confidently say that I am no stranger to meeting strangers. I have flown, driven, bussed and hitchhiked all over Canada. I have lived in cars, forts, tents, shelters, and even a storage room with my dog. With no stability or certainty in my life, I often wondered what the future would hold and how long I could stay on such a dangerous path.

After experiencing enough self-imposed pain and suffering, it was time to make a lasting change. It was time to make a change that would lead to true wealth and self-understanding.

Today, at age 35, I am an author. I have my Black Belt in Kumo Jiu Jitsu and own a successful fitness company that enhances the quality of life for hundreds of people.

I am truly inspired by the amazing team of professionals that our company employs and because of them we continue with our rapid growth. By following specific life strategies and creating a detailed investment portfolio, I have learned how to break the chains of my own self-sabotage and create TIME, HEALTH and MONEY in abundance, in my life.

I have been asked many times how I was able to so quickly make these positive and successful changes in my life.. What was my secret to change? Those questions are what inspired this book and I hope to provide some insight on the tools, strategies and techniques that I have learned.

What I was doing before wasn't working and I had to change my approach. It wasn't easy and required a lot of self-reflection. I needed some help with that and it was time to learn what I didn't know. I needed to hear what the thought leaders of the world had to say and how they looked at things. I read and listened to thousands of hours of audio content.

I admit, I went almost a decade prior without even reading one book but when I discovered the power of audio books, I went on an information gathering binge. Books, programs and sales videos became my new music. My obsessive mentality took over and I went with it. I loved hearing how these successful people thought and explained things.

As an example, I had no idea what a real asset vs a liability was, until I listened to "Rich Dad, Poor Dad". That book alone is probably why I saved my 20% down payment ($150,000) for my first 2 rental units, in less than 2 years. Robert Kiyosaki did such a great job helping me prioritize my spending habits through his book, listed in my top 14 suggested reads.

Tony Robbins, Jim Rohn, Grant Cardone, Napoleon Hill, Bedros Keullian, Michael Covel, Robert Kiyosaki, Stephen Covey, Jeffery Gitomer, Brian Tracy, Gary V and Patrick Bet David are some of my favourite authors.

The following words are a combination of the thoughts and ideas inherited from their teachings. Full credit goes to these inspiring human beings, among others. They helped me with my strategy, attitude and action. Success leaves clues for those willing to look.

What you do with your power of influence is up to you. I suggest, being ethical, being positive and being a giver. The world needs positive influencers but remember, it all starts with the ability to SELL YOURSELF FIRST.

"A journey of a thousand miles begins with one single step." Chinese proverb attrib: Laozi

STEP 1

SELL YOURSELF FIRST

S elling is a transfer of ENERGY and EMOTION or, as Tony Robbins says, "When there is rapport, whoever is the MOST certain will always influence the other". That means that CERTAINTY SELLS, so become CERTAIN of yourself first and the rest will follow.

I had to sell myself on the fact that I DESERVED to live a life on my own terms and I believe that is true for all of us. The opportunity to change our situation is always in front of us and we do have what it takes to achieve any goal.

Let's sell ourselves on accountability and taking responsibility for our actions or our inactions. Tony also mentions that, "nothing happens to us, it happens because of us". Think about that and let it sink in. I am responsible for whatever happens to me and you are responsible for whatever happens to you. We accept the good and the bad. When I started to accept that fact and resolve my inner conflict, I started to feel liberated. With the power of the most positive and constructive habits, over time, producing results, everything changed.

So, start with your own belief that you deserve to be free. Free to do what you want, when you want, with whom you want, as much as you want. To me, this is success, and I believe to the depths of my soul that I deserve it. I am CERTAINLY SOLD on my personal vision of freedom and happiness. Are you?

Be prepared to ask yourself these necessary questions. Dig deep and be honest with yourself about your vices and your values. This is the only way to carve out a lifestyle by design and stop living by chance.

These are critical times to make to critical choices because the choices we make now will set up the patterns we are destined to repeat for decades. Set yourself up for success in life by knowing the answers to these questions. What? Why? When? How?

WHAT do you want?

Know **WHAT** you want and go after it! Every success comes from a desire to achieve it – your goal and objective.

Create a vision in your mind of what you want in your life and commit yourself to action. This vision will become your focal point in life.

As the nice human being that you are, you probably want to help people. You want to make a positive impact in people's lives and go to bed at night knowing you made a difference in the world.

That's great! That is your purpose and your path. However, are you making enough money while doing it? After your monthly bills are paid and the world is saved as a result of all your hard work, did your savings grow? Are you on track to buy your first house in the next 18 months? Will you be able to take that trip for 2 to South America that you have always wanted? Will you now, finally have the time to do so?

If you answered NO to those questions, that is ok. It's a fact that majority of people make $50k per year or less…much less. After taxes, bills, and life, that doesn't leave much for planning a future in today's economy. I was that person for years and I know what it is like to work a split shift grind 7 days a week, finding myself living renewal to renewal - paycheque to paycheque - barely making it. I loved training people, though, so that kept me going… until it didn't anymore. I started burning out. The quality of my performance started to drop and it became apparent that this wasn't going to be sustainable. I was facing the choice of quitting the industry I loved or approaching things differently. I needed to change my perspective and what it meant to be effective with my time.

Listening to Tony Robbins was the first time I heard, "Where our attention goes, energy flows". That statement had a tremendous impact on me. Where was all my energy flowing? It was spent training people, listening to music, partying, cleaning the gym after clients, trying to date the wrong girls, binge watching Netflix, and every other thing that was unrelated to my financial freedom. I was investing my energy into places, people and things that were not giving me a return on my investment. I had no vision of what I wanted in my life. I was watering the weeds in my life instead of watering the seeds that had the potential to eventually bear fruit. The fruit that could hopefully sustain me on a massive level, equally, could enable me to give back to the world.

You see, once I started to ask myself WHAT I wanted, I was astonished to see what came out. Personally, I wanted time, health, family and freedom. I wanted the freedom to give back to the world on a massive level. Freedom to provide for my loved ones, and the freedom to explore the things that ignite the passion in my soul! Do you want this freedom as much as I do?

If you do, you MUST take the time to figure out the financial costs/commitments associated with this and make that your target. For me, my first goal was to increase my annual income from $35k to multiple 6 figures and to save my first $150,000. I wanted to put 20% down payment on a $700,000 house in the most beautiful city in Canada.

A house that I would rent out as an investment to grow my wealth in one of the most thriving real estate markets in Canada. This would serve as a layer in a portfolio that can continue to grow and create more wealth and TIME in my life. This was the first clearly defined target that I achieved very quickly when focused. What is yours? What is your version of the perfect life and then ask yourself…

WHY do you want it?

This question is one of the most powerful questions of all. If you do not have a reason for achieving this goal, it is just a wish or a fantasy. Why is attaining this goal even important to you? WHY do you want it? Your "WHY?" is your fuel. You need to feel the excitement burning in your heart and gut when you envision your reason for doing this. If you don't know why you want it, you don't want it.

I'm asking you to consider the time and freedom to do the things you love with the people you want to do them with. Picture whatever keeps you up at night and awakes you early with excitement. That is your "WHY?". The JOY and fulfillment that you will feel when you accomplish this, is what you need to focus on. This must be your focus when things are going your way and especially when they are not.

There is a story of a man. His wife had died early from complications in a standard operation. It wasn't common for this to happen from this procedure but it did, unfortunately and sadly. The father was left with their 2 young children and the need to support and provide for his family on a very minimal salary. The likely outcome wasn't looking good.

Having spent the past 10 years working at a local warehouse, it was very apparent that the bills were not going to get paid anymore with just his current income. He had to change his approach immediately. His reason to make a career change had transcended his comfort level. He experienced an entirely new drive to provide and to step up as a leader. So, this man took on a commission paying sales job, enjoying the idea of being responsible for exactly how much he earned. With 2 kids to send to school and bills to pay, this was his "WHY?" He focused entirely on being able to not only provide for their basic needs, but to provide a life of abundance. A life where his children, having lost their mother, could still, each be open and able to embrace the world and pursue their passions to become the best versions of themselves that they could be. He wanted them to feel loved and feel safe to grow. Ultimately, he wanted nothing more than to feel that he would have made his wife proud.

This "WHY" was so powerful, that it fuelled him to become one of the most successful influencers in the world. He ended being able to provide for many more people than just his own family. He exceeded goals in life whenever he imagined. In tapping into a passion and purpose that was bigger than him he was able to develop a source of energy to fuel his relentless drive to succeed.

Asking the question "Why?" can also help narrow down our intentions for such desires. Often, when I ask myself why I want something I can tell if it is self-serving or serving the greater good. I have noticed many times that my motives for my actions have been to satisfy selfish desires without having much impact on the collective.

Now, don't get me wrong. I am the first to admit there is a time for feeding one's ego and finding that balance will ultimately come down to your own moral compass. I'm not going to make that decision for you.

Whatever you decide as your perfect vision of a perfect life is yours to pursue. Just try to not hurt people or take away the freedoms of others. A vision where everyone can be happy is always going to help attract the power of the 'Mastermind' when it comes to building a team and family. The more we help others to get what they desire, the more likely we are to also get what we desire. It's beautiful really.

This cycle of give and take is the underlying, balancing force of the world. We see it in the trees and the magic that happens with their leaves as they recycle the very air that we breathe.

Synchronize your intentions to be focused on that which can give back and you will find no end to your power to achieve. Motivated every day to pursue your personal vision of happiness with internal peace and you will be enabled to sleep like a baby at night.

Once you know WHAT you want, WHY you want it and are SOLD on the fact that you DESERVE it there will be the need to create some urgency in life, so that real action can begin. If there is no deadline to attain, each target you set will be consumed by procrastination and distractions. Time will go by with or without you, so ask yourself this next question and hold yourself to it.

WHEN do you want it ?

"Someday…" is not a clearly defined and specific deadline. It's just not. "Someday I will have this…" or "Someday I will have that…" are terrible things to program yourself to say or think.

What day? When? The more specific you are to yourself, the easier it is to build a plan. Create urgency to achieve your goal so that you can experience the most empowering feeling in the world – i.e. the feeling of making something happen out of nothing. It's liberating and will make you want to create and do more.

7

Without urgency or pressure to achieve goals, opportunities will be missed. The power to streamline one's focus can be an incredible tool in achieving targets. Personally, I have learned that I tend to perform best when something is due immediately. Guilty of procrastination, I know all too well what it feels like to have to apply myself under extreme circumstances because of the pressure of an important deadline. The trick is to put that important deadline on yourself if you are an entrepreneur, a sales person or anyone who wants to achieve a goal. It is imperative to put a specific deadline with check points along the way. Know your projections, and know if you are projecting to hit your destination on time. Strike it while the iron is hot!

There is a story of man and woman who fell in love in high school. They would spend all their free time together. It was true love. They planned a life that included a house, kids and the ultimate dream trip to travel to South America to experience the beauty of the rainforest. To explore the Machu Pichu ruins, together, had always been their #1 dream. It was a common bond that they had shared since high school and it was a promise that they made to each other that 'someday' they would make it happen.

They worked very diligently to save for their first house. They moved in and immediately started to have kids. It was beautiful and amazing. The love and bond they all shared was as if out of a fairy tale. It was a wonderful family unity. However, these new commitments demanded financial backing. Mortgage payments, taxes, food bills, and all the other expenses that come with raising a young family, started to add up. Therefore, both parents had to work long hours just to make ends meet. They were caught in a very scary cycle and time was going by. Months turned into years and it almost seemed like the savings they thought they would 'someday' have, weren't anywhere close.

They were now getting older and the kids were almost out of the house. The eldest was in college and the youngest was 1 year away from going, as well. Once they felt certain that the kid's schooling was covered financially, they would then take time to plan the details of their dream trip and make good on their life-long promise to each other.

Just as they saw a light at the end of the tunnel, something terrible happened. The husband was diagnosed with cancer. It came out of nowhere and became the focus of their energy and money. What seemed to be a long-fought battle ended up like most cancer battles do. In tremendous suffering, pain and an empty bank account. The trip to South America never happened. 'Someday' never came.

The point of this sad story is to remind us that time IS going by, with or without us, and that we have a very short window to make good on the promises that we make to ourselves. If you want something, go after it now by clearly defining WHAT you want, WHY you want it, and WHEN you will have it. Hold yourself accountable and create a sense of urgency in your life to achieve it. There is no worse feeling than to carry around the burden of broken promises that you have made to yourself. I know from experience that this leads to blaming others and the world around you. This negative self-cycle only leads to the dark side and we don't want to become Evil Sith Sales Lords.

We want to live the momentum of one accomplishment after the other. We want to experience the tremendous feeling of fulfillment when we scratch another aspiration off our bucket list. We want to inspire those around us to also live a lifestyle by design and not by chance - by being an example. The formula is simple and clear. Know WHAT you want. Know WHY you want it and know WHEN you want it.

If you can clearly answer these questions with Passion, Purpose and Conviction, then you now feel the excitement/fear that comes with such clarity. Channel that energy to empower you and move into a mental state that urges you to push forward and never, EVER, forget your WHY.

HOW WILL YOU DO IT?

HOW Part 1 (Resolve Your Inner Conflict) Know your VICES.

I truly believe that we are a combination of Yin and Yang. I know that in my own life I most certainly have an angel on one shoulder and a devil on the other. That at any given moment I am acting out of a drive to satisfy one of those appetites.

Part of this process involves looking at those opposing forces and controlling them. Understanding that there is a time and place for both is the secret. Feed the appetites of both the Dragon and the Tiger but know that you are the master.

This means that the first step to mapping out a plan of action is to look at what has held you back in the past from accomplishing your objectives. Often we maintain a limiting belief about ourselves, or possibly a self-sabotaging pattern that we have been repeating. Then again it could be an inner conflict that we may have about the way we perceive money, relationships, addictions or patterns. I can emphatically confirm that distractions truly are the enemy of greatness.

Growing up in poverty, I never experienced a feeling of ownership of possessions or even stability. I had a bad association with money, authority and relationships. The consequence was that I wasn't attracting any success into my life.

My own limiting beliefs about myself allowed me to become addicted to everything under the sun, except success. I would quit everything that I started before I could taste any positive results. With this behaviour and pattern there was no way to stick to a plan until I re-programmed myself.

That is exactly what needs to happen. We need to RE-PROGRAM the way we spend our energy and what we think about. We can only do this by pulling the weeds from the mental garden that we have been watering, and re-planting the proper seeds.

Values

It is important to know that whatever the life goal may be, the approach should always be the same. I suggest writing down the top 5 things that are important to you. The things that you know you want to build your life around. These elements then become the only topics that we allow ourselves to focus on during the day. The only seeds that get watered by our mental and physical energy are the new SEEDS that we have planted. We call these 'VALUE SEEDS' because they are the elements that add value and joy to our lives. Avoid watering the weeds!

I recognize that values are differently defined by every person. Your priorities are for you to decide. However, here are the **VALUE SEEDS** I chose to water in my MENTAL GARDEN. I know these to be valuable to me and worth building a life around because, absent any of these elements I am an absolute disaster. Accordingly I try to water these seeds as often as I can to keep them growing strong. My personal vision of a fulfilled life is built entirely on these 5 VALUES (SEEDS).

1) The SEED of PHYSICAL HEALTH

Exercise, Proper Nutrition, and Rest all play their roles in maintaining a physically healthy body. It is imperative that I take care of my body so that I can maintain the commitments that I have made.

As an owner of a fitness centre, I can attest to the results that physical training can bring in to one's life. Maintaining a healthy fitness routine not only keeps the body moving and working correctly. It also keeps the mind clear. Proper fitness training consistently resets the internal system, enabling proper sleep and function. With these healthy habits we can be energized, pain free and able to properly perform any task.

2) The SEED of FAMILY

Spending time with the people and pets with whom I share connections is invaluable to me. Connection and Love is one of the most powerful intangibles in our world. Without connection to our community and loved ones, much of the point and purpose of life itself is lost. Therefore, contribute beyond yourself and VALUE your relationships.

Having spent a lot of time on my own, I know what it is like to be comfortable in my own skin. For many years I avoided attachments to people or pets because I thought it was a skill or strength to be free from any attachments. That was how I tried to cope. It wasn't until my heart burst wide open when I met my dog that I knew connection and relationships were important. For the first time ever I felt like I needed to protect and nurture something other than myself. This was also the last time I ever felt alone and if that is the effect a pet can have, I keenly await the arrival of my own family. The feeling of sacrificing for a child or loved one is beyond the self and truly is a spiritual drive.

3) The SEED of FREEDOM
The truth is, I don't personally care about nice clothes or acquiring possessions. I do, however, want to acquire revenue generating assets so that I do not have to work a full-time job. I am building a portfolio of passive and predictable income so that I can continue to enjoy, for myself, MORE TIME. You see, I want time to think and feel the things I choose to feel. I want to make the right decisions now so that I can eventually have the family experience that has been missing, so far, in my life. I want to have time to be there, provide for, and get to know my family. I want the freedom to move at my own pace and to smell the roses along the way - never worrying about money, time or health.

Money, fundamentally, is nothing more than a tool to build and create freedoms in our lives. It can provide the freedom to do what you want, when you want, with whom you want, as much as you want. Do not obsess over the dollar. Simply think about the FREEDOM it can bring into your life and, eventually, those around you. Learn to play the game of Capitalism and be comfortable with it. Study the people who have achieved what you are working to achieve and mirror their behaviour, because SUCCESS LEAVES CLUES. (We will be learning more about the details of the sales process in the chapters to come.)

4) The SEED of ART

Someone asked me once, what makes us different from other seemingly self-aware animals such as dolphins, whales, and chimps? My answer was, "ART". Art can be defined as our ability to express ourselves and our feelings through creative means. By appealing to our many senses we can explore the multiple energies that come when we connect with a special piece of art. I find it fascinating that the need for ART in our lives seems to transcend Maslow's hierarchy of human needs. Love of ART addresses the potentials of the needs of the spirit.

For example, the feeling of painting a beautiful picture, or writing a song that perfectly encapsulates the feeling of a broken heart - these are connections to the spirit. These are moments where we are feeling something bigger than ourselves. These moments are crucial for our spiritual growth and to confirm that we are connected.

Writing, talking, singing, dancing, painting, drawing, playing musical instruments – these are all great examples of how we connect with inspiration and can release it back into the world. Art is a TOOL to help build diversity and compassion within our hearts. I urge us all to connect with our inner artist. It truly is our higher self.

5) The SEED of COMMUNITY

The power of the collective is still unmeasured and often overlooked. When people connect harmoniously and share in a vision, the most incredible things can happen. We see that power in sports teams, creative teams, bands, communities, towns and cities. Collective power succeeds, in part, because we are a pack species. We need to feel connected to each other. Solitary confinement, as a punishment, even when it involves being separated from people who don't like each other, is nevertheless particularly painful. The pain of separation and isolation is significant punishment for any human being.

If we value the people in our community as extended family members there will be a shift in our perception of those in our community. Harness the power of the Mastermind by staying open, receptive and compassionate to those around us and in our community. If everybody is playing the right instrument, we can make beautiful music that can help make a positive impact on the world in ways yet undiscovered.

The secret is to understand that we, in one way or another, truly are the average of most of the people we spend our time with. Surround yourself with people who inspire you to grow and become your best. Hang out with people who are better than you at the things you want in your life. This will encourage you to raise your standards. Skills, thoughts, finances, passions, insights etc. are things worth accepting from people. Create a community of people with similar outlooks and engage with them.

Putting It All Together

These 4 elements of Health, Family, Freedom and Art, make me the man I am today. By watering and nurturing even ONLY these seeds, they grew roots. Strong deep roots that will continue to grow until my family and community can eat the fruits that they bear. In this way we give back to the world on such a SUSTAINABLE LEVEL.

Considering these 4 ELEMENTS, I'm reminded of the story of the Samurai. They were dedicated to mindfulness with everything that they did. From sunrise to sunset, everything was thought through in order to serve the productive use of their time and energy. Whatever they were doing, that is where they were. The Samurai knew what they valued, and approached life with complete dedication.

They valued their health, maintaining a very clean and consistent diet of the foods that they harvested themselves. With such grace in their meal preparation it was a thing of beauty to watch them perform something as simple as serving tea. With an almost ceremonious and artistic flare to everything they did, this culture of warriors lived present and grounded.

The consistency in their physical training regimen was, and still is, of such a standard that only the most dedicated can maintain its requirements. Pursuing strength, power, agility, purpose, and endurance was at the forefront of the Samurai training. Being the founders of Japanese Jiu Jitsu, the Samurai studied and set a standard in the way of the body that still only few can attain.

To grow, protect and provide for a family was the highest honour for a Samurai. They built and shared beautiful villages and communities, taking care of one another while honouring the Bushido code. That code of loyalty, courage, veracity, compassion and honour is important. The code requires that an appreciation for life is needed in order to add balance to one's character.

No matter how full a day was, a Samurai warrior always took time to meditate, do calligraphy, write a Zen poem or perhaps draw a picture of nature's beauty. Whatever it was, it was a moment of tranquility and connection. Sitting with gratitude and grace will always lead to inspiration.

The Samurai were warriors who fought a different War than the War we are fighting today, but the principles of War are the same. Freedom requires resources, resilience, and a relentless STRATEGY.

HOW PART 2 (Strategy and Execution)

Now that we have faced our inner demons, eliminated our limiting beliefs and all the baggage we have been carrying, it is time to charge forward with a plan of action. However, we need a plan that is logical, clear and possible. The art of professional Selling (Sales) is a great reference point for completely understanding this concept, because it is all about the numbers and the results. The numbers and results don't lie. Find the effective and successful formula and stick to it.

For example, if you want to make $100,000 this year, just reverse engineer from that number. $8,333 per month for 12 months is what that is. This is also, is $2,083 per week. If you make $200 commission on each sale, that is basically 2 deals per day (on a 5-day work week). If you are closing 50% of your leads, you need 4 showing appointments. If only 50% of your appointments show, you need 8 appointments per day. If you book 50% of your contacts, you need to make 16 Contacts per day to make $100,000 this year.

There it is. A quick example of how numbers work and will always work. It just comes down to making your plan and holding yourself accountable to it.

Let's look at another example of designing your own life. Write down on a piece of paper what you want your life to be like in 10 years. The more specific that you can be, the better will be the result. Write down all of the details that get you pumped, excited and energized for the future. Think about your home, family, time, hobbies, arts, passions etc. Everything you want your life to be about in 10 years is to be written and recorded now. I urge you to really take the time and do this exercise. Be honest and be real about how much free time you want, how healthy you want to be, how much money you want to have invested, what your portfolio will look like, how many kids you want to have, the morals/values you will share with your spouse, and everything else that feels good to you.

Now, on the next piece of paper, write down with the same detail, your 5-year vision. Be specific and make sure it aligns with the 10-year plan. Again, the more specific you are able to be, the better will be the outcome. The friends, the pets, and the experiences, etc., you want be having, are all detailed in this 5-year plan.

Follow this same blueprint for your 3 year, 2 year, 1 year, 6 months, 3 months, 1 month, 1 week, and 1 day plan. If you accurately and honestly want to pursue the 10-year vision, then you should be able to connect the dots that you just laid out. Take these pages and put them somewhere where you will always see them. Hold yourself accountable to these steps by staying focused and resourceful. This is your map. A logical and clear plan of action to which you are committed - that you are sold on.

Now that you are committed to the fact that you deserve what you want, sold on why you want it, sold on when you are going to have it and sold on the steps/finances you need to make it a reality, it is time to generate revenue. It is time to influence and sell others on your certainty. It is time to help enough people get what they want. It will then inevitably follow that you will get what you want.

Step 1 Review Questions

Take time to write down your answers to the following questions and put them somewhere that you will be reminded of them every day.

1) What is your idea of a perfect life? (Clearly define income, friends, hobbies, relationships, places, and the skills that you need and want).
2) Why do you want to achieve this? (Think about the joy, freedom and happiness it will bring.)
3) When do you want to achieve this? (Be specific with days, months, and years.)
4) What are your VICES?
5) What are your VALUES?
6) How much money do you want to save this year?
7) How much money do you need to save each month to achieve what you answered in question 6?
8) How much money do you need to make each month to save what you answered in question 7?
9) How many sales per day do you need to sell to make the amount answered in question 7?

EMBODY THE SALES PROCESS

Learn it, Live it and Love it!

What does it mean to embody something? According to dictionary.com, the definition of 'embody' is "to express, personify, or exemplify in concrete form". That is amazing really. To express, personify and exemplify something is a powerful and very committed state.

What is 'sales'?

The ABC's of sales - Always Be Closing - is a marketing term as old as marketing itself. Always closing is exactly what we are always doing. We are living a life with an open heart and open mind, always embracing every opportunity. We are aiming to make a difference in people's lives on a massive level and we must have a passion to help as many people as possible.

Understanding that LIFE IS SALES, is how we embody the sales process. We must understand and know that every exchange and interaction is a sale. Every thought- exchange, gesture and body language expression, is a part of the sales process. We are always buying or selling ideas, rumors, lessons, services, products, and opinions from each other, all the time.

Babies learn to sell their mothers on getting what they want instinctively and are great at selling. They cry and, almost immediately, they get can get fed, hugged, massaged or gratified. If they are unsuccessful, what happens? They cry louder! They ask for the sale again. They don't take 'no' for an answer and they are persistent. Babies are great persuaders – great sales people.

Selling doesn't stop as babies. We're just getting started. We grow up, notice the opposite sex, and as kids, we start to market ourselves to each other. Powerful marketing strategies start to be deployed. Social proof is a common marketing tool we discover when young. The pretty girls usually notice the popular boys first, and vice versa. If everybody else likes them, so should they. Social proof is powerful and used in all successful mainstream media marketing campaigns.

Dating is also about sales. Subtly or not so subtly, we can see people on their dates selling each other on their own features and benefits. Appearance, accomplishments, hobbies, and values are ways that we try to promote ourselves to persuade the other person to be with us. It is common to see how people use this 'Mirroring' technique to create an affinity between them. As they find common ground to share and build rapport, we can see people agreeing to go see or go do things that they wouldn't usually do, just to spend time with each other. When they sit at a restaurant or bar, they share the same body language. Their eyes, their shoulders, their vocal tonality, and their distance will tend to unify them in style and substance. This is mirroring and it happens when people are building a rapport. It can be conscious or unconscious, but it is happening. It is a powerful, and often instinctive, sales tool.

The selling does not stop Here. Parents try to sell their kids on which morals are good for them and which values they should represent. The kids will ultimately decide if they are buying or not. Should they choose to object, the parent then starts the process of overcoming objections. Overcoming objections is one of the scariest and most intimidating things to have to execute with a stranger, but we do it all the time with people that we trust. It is just a matter of perspective.

Sometimes we are the seller and sometimes we are the buyer. This is how we embody the sales process. Understanding the balanced cycle of giving and getting is what this is about. I love getting sold if it is a service, a product or a way of thinking that adds value to my life. I love when I am convinced of something of which I wasn't previously convinced.

We can see that we are surrounded by selling, influencing, persuading, inspiring, and leading each other all the time. Society needs thought leaders, teachers, motivators, influencers persuaders and sellers, so that we can continue to evolve. The important thing is to determine which are the most productive services, products, thoughts or ideas. Only buy or sell the ideas, services and products that add value to your life and the world around you.

Selling fitness is fantastic because it has me always looking for the opportunity to help somebody. Directly enhancing the quality of people's lives is the purpose of my company and everywhere I look, I see someone who could benefit from our services. As fitness professionals, we can have an emotional and physical impact on the people we get to work with. How many people do you see in a day that could benefit from your services?

Your answer to that question is probably "EVERYONE!", and that is most likely true if you are good at your job. You're also wondering now, how to get these people converted into paying clients. In fact, that is also why you bought this book. So, now that you are a walking motivator you can see that the world is abundant with the opportunity to help people and the need to always be ready to close. Let start funnelling them into your business and changing lives.

The 5-step conversion process starts with understanding the Suspect to Community Member transformation process that must happen in order to grow your business.

Here are the 5 stages of this conversion process.

Stage 1) Suspect
Stage 2) Prospect
Stage 3) Customer
Stage 4) Client
Stage 5) Community Member

The following explains in detail the funnelling and conversion process. Using my experience and knowledge accumulated over the years, I will try to help you learn from my mistakes and have a better understanding of what it takes to convert a Suspect to a long-term Community Member.

Who is a Suspect?

Everyone is a Suspect! Anyone who would benefit from your service or product is a Suspect. In fitness and wellness, that is basically everybody. A suspect is a potential future client who may or may not yet know it. It is your job as a salesperson to attract and keep their attention. To appeal to a Suspect is at the forefront of basic marketing. Sometimes it is not easy to turn heads and create an inquiry. Most people are so consumed with their thoughts and patterns that they probably won't just walk in and order your best service. You need to attract them with marketing. Some of the ways we do this are with Special offers, colours, sounds, social proof, consistency, authority, energy and enthusiasm.

Who is a Prospect?

Once we have successfully attracted the attention, curiosity and intrigue of a Suspect, they then become a Prospect. A Prospect is anybody who has made an inquiry into your product or service. An inquiry could be as obvious as a walk in, call in or message. Or it could be something less obvious, such as a like/comment on a FB post. Either way, it is someone showing interest in what you are selling. It is your duty as a salesperson to show at least the same interest and attention in return.

Prospecting is the process of marketing to our demographic. To do this, we need to know where these people are. We call this '**lead sourcing**'. In this we identify the source of possible leads as the first step to prospecting. Knowing where leads come from is crucial. Where do prospects spend their time? Who do they talk to? Which websites do they frequent?

Lead Sources

Some examples of common lead sources are:

- The Internet (Facebook, Google, Groupon)
- Word of Mouth (Referrals)
- Location and Signage (Walk in traffic)
- Outreach (Cold Calling and Door Knocking)
- Lunch and Learns (corporate presentations)
- Reactivations (Former clients returning)
- Lead Boxes (Ballet boxes to collect contact info)
- Welcome Wagon (greeting service)

I know that there are many more lead sources than the ones just listed. However, this is to get your mind thinking in the right direction about lead sources and where prospects may be coming from. Use your own creativity to come up with campaigns that may work for your business. The important part is to know which sources are consistently generating leads and which are not. You might find that 80 % of your prospects are coming from 20% of your sources. In which case, scale it by focusing on the 20% with 80% of your resources.

Campaigns

Once you have decided on which lead sources to focus your resources on, it is time to create a campaign. The purpose of the sales campaign is to convert Suspects into Prospects. Capturing the attention, imagination, and inspiration of the Suspect is what a good marketing campaign does. A great one however, not only gets the attention but also has a 'call to action'. A 'call to action' encourages the Suspect to "buy now", "message now", "call now", or "download now". The 'call to action' is for the Suspect to take the next step and make an inquiry and therefore, become a Prospect.

Having a campaign going for every lead source is good preparation and will always increase the chances of campaign success. Find out what works online for you. Find out what works to generate referrals from existing members and be ready to launch your campaigns at specific days and times. Design your campaigns and be diligent about working them. Consistency is the name of this game.

A successful campaign will always generate leads and prospects. It is ok if you barely break even on the front-end cost of the marketing investment. That means that your discounted offer may have produced some leads, but may or may not have covered all of the money spent on the campaign. This is ok because if you close a couple of those sales after the intro, that is where you make the money. The profit is on the back end through the renewal and referrals.

PEOPLE are PREDICTABLE

I have learned that people tend to live their lives in cycles. There are predictable patterns and repetitions that a successful influencer can identify and plan around. In the fitness industry, for example, this effect is ever prevalent at the end of a comfort zone when people are ready to make healthy choices. The obvious ones are January and September. The 2 busiest months of the year for us always follow the slowest times (Aug and Dec). We can see examples of this throughout the year. On a smaller scale people behave this way after long weekends and even after regular weekends. We see this on Mondays, when the gym is at its busiest. We call it 'guilty Monday' because people seem to feel guilty for their indulgences on the weekend, only to repeat the same pattern again by Friday.

Knowing this about target markets is very important in deciding when to launch campaigns. Don't waste time, energy and marketing dollars and remember that timing is everything. Avoid 'winging' it by researching when particular markets make buying decisions, and then strike while the iron is hot.

FUNNELS and PIPELINES

If a campaign is successful, it has produced Prospects. These Prospects have now been funnelled from the campaign into pipelines. The goal now is to always keep the pipelines full of opportunity. Track and record Prospect's appointments and where they are in the pipeline. Did they cancel? Did they rebook? What day is follow-up required? Keep your pipelines full, staying with them with consistency and enthusiasm.

Facebook

Since the arrival of Facebook it is amazing to see what has happened in the world of free markets and capitalism. The little guy has a chance now because the playing field has levelled out. Anyone can succeed if they have the passion, the product, the purpose and the patience to follow the process.

As of the fourth quarter of 2016, Facebook had **1.86 billion** monthly active users. That is absolutely staggering, considering that to get a fraction of that statistic watching a commercial on television would cost hundreds of thousands of dollars. Now, using the advertising tools provided by a Facebook business account, the options are endless. The power to target who, where, when, what and how people are exposed to our content, is at our fingertips.

The most miraculous part of using Facebook is the instant connections and interactions that can happen once the Suspect becomes a Prospect. Through instant messages, comments, likes and shares we are able to convert these Prospects into Customers and eventually Community Members.

For example, in the fitness industry I run a lot of campaigns on Facebook that require our suspects to 'Like' and Comment/Message to receive an awesome gift or discount. The moment that they do that, they have become a Prospect and they have now taken the first step to making a positive change in their lives. It is my duty to ensure that their needs are met by using my product or service. I do this by responding instantly. People purchase with emotion, and, like anything, emotions change. If they are feeling your vibe now, then you must respond immediately and keep the vibe alive.

LIKES, FANS and EMAIL LISTS

The power of a following is often overlooked in business. How many people can hear your voice, consistently? Through the power of social media, we can access millions of people if we create a loud voice. That is, if we are willing to promote and put it out there.

Creating online funnels to capture emails or attract 'likes', is what we are always need to be doing and there are many simple funnels that can be made or bought. Once followers are attracted and registered, Bedros Keullian teaches that we must indoctrinate them with content. We must create a feeling that we are the authority and that we know best when it comes to an idea, service or product. People buy from the 'authority' because they know the 'authority' has the best expertise.

Free giveaways are the usually the best way to attract a Suspect to opt in and provide their email or 'like' your page. A free gift-card, a discount, a book, or a product giveaway in return for a 'follow' is a great way to build a lead list. If someone has 'liked' a post on a FB business page, we can then see an option to invite them to 'like' your page. Run ads that ask for a 'like' and 'comment'. This will ensure that they are encouraged to 'follow' you and a 'comment' will open lines of communication. Now we have converted a Suspect into a Prospect. Our new Prospects might not bite immediately. However, they are already tasting the sizzle. If you are consistent with your content, they will bite eventually to test and taste the steak.

Outreach

Outreach marketing is as old as the dinosaurs. Outreach is the process of cold calling and door knocking. I have learned that there is still excellent value and power in the personal approach.

With fitness sales, I have found the personal approach easy because I know that everyone, in some way, could benefit from our service. The secret is to have something to offer at the outset, invoking the law of reciprocity.

For example, a successful strategy is in the distribution of $100 gift cards. It may seem that this is too much to give away. The rationale is that our product range does not include a 'stand-alone' $100 product, so the gift card simply represents a realistic discount in the eventual purchase of a more valuable product. The Gift Card was the trigger and motivation to create the interest to book an appointment. Giving the card gets the lead.

So, in this example of 'outreach' we engage the ability simply to walk up to a person and become part of their reality for a brief moment. It takes certainty and Jedi-like mind control for outreach to be effective but these strategies are proven to be tried, tested and true. Everything depends on the level of motivation to succeed and the priorities that drive those motivations.

I remember when I first moved to Victoria BC. I was 23 years old and had no money. I had had some luck selling fitness memberships in Toronto so I imagined continuing to build on that experience in Victoria. It was June 2014 and Planet Fitness was the gym at which I chose to make my first presentation. Heading into summer, they weren't exactly handing out jobs, so I requested that they give me a chance with a commission only sales position. They had nothing to lose because I was going to generate my own leads as well. All I needed from them was a ballet pad, 1 lead box and a small table.

I took these items down to an outside courtyard where it was sunny and pleasant. I strategically placed the table with the lead box at a point that covered the entrances of a bank, a coffee shop and a grocery store. My placement was perfect. I was campaigning to a constant flow of walking traffic. I approached everybody, and I do mean everybody. I offered free trial memberships, PT sessions and consultations to whomever I could get to enter my 'free draw'. I was a walking lead box. It was awesome!

After 4 hours of hustling I had acquired more than 100 leads, names and numbers of people who had shown even the slightest glimpse of interest in my product. I ate a big meal, slammed an energy drink and went immediately to phone work. I called everyone, without delay, offering an incentive of a discounted rate and a free trial. The discount was minor and the free trial was necessary to motivate action. The tactics were entirely legitimate and straightforward. With urgency and excitement in my tone I booked 90% of the people I spoke to and now I also had a lead list to work.

The 'salespeople' who were on a base pay and employed by Planet Fitness seemed threatened and they didn't know what to think of this crazy guy from Toronto. They could sense that something was about to change around there, and change it certainly did.

Booking Appointments

Booking appointments must be done with excitement and a keen interest in meeting a Prospect's needs.

I begin by asking a couple quick questions and then proceed to book an appointment to meet in person so that the Prospect can claim their introductory offer. The offer is usually represented as a low barrier introduction that will enable initial product experience without the requirement of a significant commitment. A free session or a few sessions for a discounted price, usually do the job to get someone to commit to an appointment.

When booking the appointments do not ask questions that invite 'yes' or 'no answers. Keep the conversation flowing and open and avoid the roadblocks that can bring the flow of thoughts to an end. It's important to create the opportunity, in this conversation, to explain how life-enhancing the product and experience will be.

For example, if the conversation pitch is "Mrs. Robinson, that is great that you are ready to take the next step in bettering your health! I am very excited to find out how we can best meet your needs. Can you come in this week?" she can simply say "No", followed by some schedule or time objection.

When booking the appointment, it is important to use gated questioning. That means questions that involve choosing an option, and not a 'yes' or a 'no'. Remember, at this point the conversation is with a person who is barely a Prospect. They could swim away at any second, so don't make that an easy option. Do keep the interest bubbling as you move the conversation down your funnel and into your pipeline.

So, a more successful example of working to book an appointment would include and present a few choices. "Mrs. Robinson, that is great that you are ready to take the next step in bettering your health! I am very excited to find out how we can best meet your needs. Are you more interested in Group Training or Personal Training? Also, which day this week works best to get started? Do prefer Monday, Tuesday or Wednesday AM or PM?"

Notice, when phrased like that, the correct response to that question is one of those three options. The response of 'no' is not invited as an answer and would also be socially awkward. Therefore Mrs. Robinson has been walked through a gate. This process continues with the booking of a time as well as a date certain. For example, close in this way. "OK Mrs. Robinson, that's great! On Tuesday I have 9 am, Noon or 5 pm. Which works better for you?"

Tonality

A statistical study of note from Bob Birdwhistle, and Albert Mehrabian (Kinesics & Communication) is interesting and relevant. Both studied non- verbal communication and introduced the following assessment. (Note Mehrabian has summarized his works and the work of some others in his book 'Silent Messages')

The study reported that 55% of communication is BODY LANGUAGE, 38% is TONALITY and 7% is VERBAL. It is fascinating that communication comprises only 7 % of what we say and the rest is how we say it.

For example, you will notice how friends who are happy to see each other typically greet with higher octaves, but when sad to say goodbye they end up using lower tones. It is noticeable when an individual is happy or encouraging of another, they will use higher tones.

It is also true that if an individual is angry or discouraging, lower tones will be used. This is interesting to us because, using the same words, yet with different tones, we can observe and imagine very different responses.

When researching the topic of tonality, I stumbled upon a joke told by Sales Guru, Greg Woodley.

"You see there was this unfortunate man who broke the law and went to prison. He was feeling very scared his first night alone in his cell.

After the lights went out he heard one of the other inmates in a cell quite a long way off shout out "32". Then all the prisoners burst out laughing. When the laughter subsided, he heard another inmate call out "66". Once again this was followed by a burst of laughter. This went on for some time before they all fell to sleep.

The man was intrigued by this behavior.

The next morning during breakfast in the eating area the man gathered up his courage and spoke to one of the older prisoners and asked him what was going on.

The older inmate said, "Many of us have been in here for a long time. There's not much you can do when the lights go out. So, to amuse ourselves we tell jokes. But after a while we all seemed to know all the jokes, so it became easier to just give the jokes a number and just shout out the number rather than taking all that time to tell the joke."

Ahhh. Now it all made sense.

So, for the next few weeks, the man listened to the numbers and found out what joke corresponded to what number and which numbers got the biggest laughs.

Finally, one night he decided to join in. After about five or six jokes had been told "by the numbers". He shouted out "22!" Nothing happened? Dead silence. He thought that maybe the others didn't hear him. So, he waited till a few more jokes were numbered and shouted out, as loud as he could, "66!" Again, just silence? This happened to him about five times.

The next morning, he just had to find out why no one laughed at his numbers. He went to the old man again and asked him. "Why does no one laugh at my jokes?"

The old man replied, "Ah, it's the way you tell them."

Confirming Appointments

Now that we have elegantly and efficiently booked our prospect with a day and time that we know works for them, do not count on them to show up. In fact, I have often witnessed an entire day of 10 booked sales appointments - all NO SHOWS.

This is often the case with fitness sales, probably because our Prospects need our help to get in shape and that involves creating new routines. Showing up to see a Personal Trainer isn't exactly the typical Tuesday routine for Mrs. Robinson. She is most likely nervous and looking for any reason to not show.

If appointments are confirmed the day/night before, the show-up ratios will go up and the chances of success will significantly increase. Again avoid 'yes' or 'no questions such as, "Are we still on tomorrow?" Or "Do you still want to get started?" Mrs. Robinson can simply say "no", followed by an objection. Again, we've killed the deal.

I have learned that a friendly reminder tends to help keep the interest. For example, a text message the night before that says "See you tomorrow! 303 Douglas St." or "I am excited to meet you tomorrow! Don't forget a bottle of water. J". These quick little messages are just enough to remind that someone has set time aside and that there is a sense of accountability that comes with having a Personal Trainer.

Be diligent with your confirmations because the salespeople who stick to the steps, and do not break stride, are the ones who end up increasing their chances of success. Remember, it is a numbers game. Your booking and show ratios will determine how many people are presented with your product or service and ultimately this factor will determine the growth of any business.

3 QUICK TIPS for BOOKING APPOINTMENTS

Stay within 10 days. Any appointment booked more than 10 days ahead will have a greater chance of being cancelled or becoming a 'no-show'.

Avoid yes or no questions. Don't invite the opportunity for your Prospect to say no.

1) Use strategic reminders. Send an email 3 days before the appointment describing what to expect, and a text of your address the night before explaining how excited you are to anticipate the meeting.

Who is a CUSTOMER?

The first time that a Prospect buys what you are selling is when they actually graduate to becoming a Customer. A Prospect will only buy what you are selling when they have been inspired and motivated. To convert from Prospect to Customer, we need to understand the buying motives of our Prospect. People buy with emotion and back up with logic. That means, to make a buying decision, the Prospect must feel something emotionally in order to justify any buying decision.

What do buyers feel? What do they want to feel? Why are they buying? Why are they not buying? How long have they been feeling this way? When do they want to feel different? We are now asking our Prospect the same questions we asked of our self in step 1. We ask these questions so that we can accurately assess and meet our Prospect's needs. The first step is one of Prospect qualification.

The Prospect to Customer conversion is a very intricate and detailed process. This is very much the 'meat' of this book and the main reason that you bought, read or are listening to this program. Pay particular attention to the next lessons because if you master Building Rapport, Qualifying, Gated Questioning, Need Analysis, Creating Value, Overcoming Objections, Presenting, Pricing, Closing and Post Closing, you will be an unstoppable seller.

Rapport

All professional sales training advice books stress how important establishing rapport is in the sales process. Trusting, Comfortable, Relaxed, and Receptive are all words that help describe the state of a rapport. What we do to connect and build affinity with our prospects will determine how strong will be their affinity as a customer.

When establishing rapport, remember that people like people who are like themselves. Prospective customers need to feel that their needs, perspectives, values and principles are understood and shared. People especially like their friends to have common interests, so be sure to create a friendly trusting environment.

Bedros Keullian talks a lot about becoming an assistant buyer in the eyes of the Prospect. Allow your Prospect to feel that your sincerity is coming from an authentic place. We do this by asking real questions, almost personal questions, that only a friend could ask. In combination with tonality and body language, these questions are very effective in building rapport.

According to the professional sales author, Mike Shultz, there are 7 points to remember when building rapport.

1) Be genuine
2) Be warm and friendly
3) Show interest
4) Don't seem needy
5) Give genuine compliments
6) Calibrate the rapport to "just right"
7) Read the culture and adapt

Qualifying

Qualifying is the process of gathering information so that you, as the salesperson, can match the Prospect with the best suited option.

Qualifying a Prospect consists of exploring their budget, schedule, personal and social circumstances, location, and most importantly, their need/want. This is the part of the presentation that will prepare you for an easy close or a lot of frustration. Much depends on how elegant and confident you are in asking these questions. These questions are designed to answer the potential and the inevitable objections.

The most common questions and objections we will often face when selling are related to location, schedule, spouse and money. There are other objections, of course, that we face as sales people. Selling is not an exact science. However, the idea to overcome any objection is the same. For learning and teaching purposes, we will focus on these major objections.

According to Sales Master, David Masover on davidmasover. com, there are 3 things that apply in order that any Prospect is enabled to buy.

The 3 things that MUST apply for a Prospect to be qualified are:

1) That the Prospect has a current, relevant need/want or desire.
2) That the Prospect has the time, money or resources to commit.
3) That the person you are talking to has the power to make buying decisions.

If your Prospect meets all 3 of these qualifications, you are ready to rock!

Here are some sample qualifying questions that I have used in the fitness industry to qualify prospects. The approach can be modified and adapted to many other industries but always the principles are the same.

Know the potential objections and close them without the prospect realizing. When successfully closing the gates, the only topic left will be cost and value. We will discuss these important topics in the "Needs Analysis" portion of this guide.

QUALIFYING QUESTIONS and CLOSING THE GATES

These are questions to be asked before isolating the specific goals or needs. We want to get these basics out of the way so that they don't reappear, unanswered, when the process has moved to more detailed and final presentation. Close these gates so that the Prospect is unable to back-track and contradict them self. The key is to be elegant and make sure that there is good communication and rapport with the Prospect throughout the qualifying process.

1) "I'm very happy you made it in today Mrs. Robinson. Did you find the facility and parking ok? Is this location convenient for you?"

2) "Part of what we are doing today Mrs. Robinson, is designing a game plan and strategy that will work for your routine of life. What is your schedule like? Do you prefer to exercise in the AM or PM?"

3) "What is it that you do for a living Mrs. Robinson? Are you seated most of the day at a desk or do you get to move around? "

4) "Does your husband know that you are here to see a Personal Trainer today and is he encouraging of you to better your health?"

5) If the answer was yes, follow that up with "Great, so I guess it is safe to say you have the power to make your own buying decisions - correct?"

Did you notice that by asking these 5 questions, we have determined that her location is good, her schedule is good, and that she has demonstrated that she has adequate income. Mrs. Robinson has also shared with us that she has the power to make buying decisions.

Now, is the moment when we take this process an important step further and determine her ultimate need reason for being with us. Mrs. Robinson has a problem, a need, a want or a desire that has led her to approach this far into your funnel. It is time to meet those needs and become the solution she has been searching for. If we can meet Mrs. Robinson's true need, she will buy and become a customer.

How do we meet a Prospect's needs? I have learned that most people don't readily volunteer such information. They may say that they have a goal to lose weight but that isn't necessarily their need. Why do they want to lose weight? How is that going to feel to them? How long have they imagined to sharing this goal and need? These are things we need to find out about Mrs. Robinson if we want to inspire her trust.

This process is identical to the process of selling yourself that we discussed in step 1 except, we are now helping our Prospect with their 'What, Why, and When?' It is imperative our Prospect opens up and is forthcoming about their reasons for seeking help and services. Questions, questions, and more questions will always provide the answers. Once the prospect's 'true need' is disclosed and established, the job of meeting the need and solving the problem can begin.

Here are examples, in the fitness industry, of the questions I would ask to help determine the most suitable program for any individual.

Need Analysis
(What, Why, When, Where, How)

1) "Tell me Mrs. Robinson, **what** brings you here today? Do you have a performance, appearance or lifestyle goal?"
2) "That's a wonderful goal! We are specialists in just that. **Why** do you want to do this?"

3) "Fantastic! **When** do you want to do this?"
4) "On a scale of 1 -10, 10 being of top importance, **where** does this goal sit on your personal priority scale?"
5) "Ok, that sounds good. I am excited to help design a plan with you. **How** long have you been thinking about this?"

Ask these 5 questions and more. Always keep your questioning directed to the task at hand i.e. isolating the expressed need. Defining the 'need' is critical so remain very focused. Don't become distracted. According to Jordan Belfort's (The original Wolf of Wall Street), straight-line persuasion principles, it is important to go from AàB as smoothly, elegantly and efficiently as possible. In this situation, A à B is transitioning from Prospect to Customer.

Follow the steps and stick to your script of questions. Eventually, it will become second nature to ask these gated questions. Guiding your prospect toward their objective is your duty as a leader, seller, parent, motivator, persuader or influencer.

Mirroring

Mirroring is a technique used to engage body language. Remember that people like people who are like themselves? Without being obvious and awkward, simply try and mirror the Prospect's physical styles. Be subtle. When the Prospect is leaning back in a chair, mirror that relaxed gesture. If they lean forward with their hands on the table, join them in the behavior. Again, be subtle. Be casual and smooth. After some time, test the rapport and initiate the next move by adjusting your chair or, perhaps, rubbing your hands. If your action is followed by something of a similar action, there is successful rapport and connection.

This unconscious 'copy-cat' behavior is called limbic synchrony and it is hard-wired into the human brain. Carol Kinsey Goman describes it well in her article 'The Art and Science of Mirroring' published in Forbes Magazine May 2011. She writes;

"Babies do it even before birth; their heartbeats and body functions take on a rhythm that matches those of their mothers. As adults, we do it when we are talking with someone we like, are interested in, or agree with. We subconsciously switch our body posture to match that of the other person – mirroring that person's nonverbal behavior and signaling that we are connected and engaged."

Goman also adds an example of a recent study on Mirroring.

"Volunteers were (ostensibly) asked for their opinions about a series of advertisements. A member of a research team mirrored half the participants, taking care not to be too obvious. A few minutes later, the researcher 'accidentally' dropped six pens on the floor. Participants who had been mimicked were two to three times more likely to pick up the pens. The study concluded that mimicry had not only increased good will toward the researcher (in a matter of minutes), but also prompted an increased social orientation in general."

Become aware of these gestures, signs and indicators. They are always providing insight into our Prospects.

Add Value

Now is the time to remember the '5 Value Seeds' that were planted in Step 1 Anything that adds to the growth of those seeds adds value and becomes a reason to make a purchase. We will always pay for true value. If an idea, product, or service enhances the Prospect's desire a purchase will follow. Value is very much about perception and is unique to every individual.

Be the Golden Pill

When discussing value, I always turn to the story of the Golden Pill.

If there was, truly, a Golden Pill that had been proven to eliminate and prevent all forms of disease, keeping your hair healthy, your skin vibrant, your muscles full, and all with 0% surplus body fat, would you take the Golden Pill? There will be no negative side effect and it only needs to be taken once in a lifetime. Would you still take it? The only catch is - it costs $250,000. Would you STILL take it? Maybe not, at least until you had the money. It's a fair guess that many people would save their money with the objective of looking to happily invest $250,000 into the Golden Pill. It would add value and meet needs.

The art of presenting an idea, service or product is to create the intense certainty, within the mind of the Prospect, that you ARE the Golden Pill. Create the belief by your Prospect that they have finally found the answer to their quest or problem. Work to create a perception of so much 'value' that the price seems too good to be true. When value is created, price is no longer an issue, and deals get closed. Be the Golden Pill and always work to add 'value'.

Presenting

Once the Prospect's 'What, Why, When, Where, and How' have been established a convincing presentation must follow. The presentation of the idea, service or product must resonate with the Prospect. Remember, you are the Golden Pill, and this must be a golden presentation. Be a pro and be prepared. Know the order of the process and be conscious of the questions you are asking.

A clear idea of the Prospect's needs must align, with absolute perfection and certainty, with the product, service or idea, that you are presenting. Know the product, know the features, know the benefits, and most importantly, know when to mention the most correct and relevant features.

For example, in the fitness industry many women express goals related to weight loss and lifestyle. They say that they want to lose body fat, get sweaty, be social, have fun and have time for themselves. Many feel that they are always taking care of everyone except themselves. So, when presenting to Mrs. Robinson, encourage her get her sweaty and to get her muscles a little bit shaky. Encourage her to get some adrenaline flowing, possibly finishing with 5 minutes of a quick boxing session. This can be fun, sweaty, empowering and energetic. Exactly what she feels she wants and needs.

She doesn't want to sit and hear about her posterior chain. She might need that, and it can be worked into the training, but it should not be included in the presentation. Mrs. Robinson wants to experience the feelings that she's imagining that training will bring and that is what she can receive in the presentation - an actual experience of value. It's something that she can't do on her own and therefore will readily pay for.

Attitude

Your presentation must have energy and enthusiasm. You must be passionate about what you are selling. You can't be deceptive because we humans have built in lie detectors. We can sense uncertainty in any individual. Be clear, confident and certain of your idea, service or product, but, always remain able to adapt to the requirements of individual personalities. Be a chameleon but always stick to the principles of qualifying, need analysis and the creation of value.

Maintaining a positive attitude for every sales appointment can be tough. A true test of character can be defined by the ability to cope with rejection positively, constructively and successfully. We must be able to move forward despite setbacks.

In 2014, Walter Rogers wrote an article titled 'Maintaining a Winning Attitude' In this article he talks about Bob and Amanda.

"Bob and Amanda both had the same situation: 200 calls and no appointments. Bob believed this meant there was no opportunity for him and no option but to fail, so he was ready to quit. However, Amanda, rather than blaming the economy or the prospects, believed this to be a temporary slump that could be rectified by changing her approach. To her, the situation represented an opportunity to succeed by learning something new, so she got right to work on a new strategy.

Celebrated peak-performance expert Tony Robbins would say that Amanda has learned to "tell herself a different story" about her situation and her options. Bob looked at his slump and told himself that he was going to fail. Amanda looked at her slump and told herself that if she would change her strategy and learn to do some things differently, her chances of success would go way up. It isn't hard to predict which story will have the happier ending."

Test Closing

During any presentation, we are elegantly using techniques to 'test the close'. We want to find out if we are on the right track and how close we are to our desired result. We do this with more questions.

For example, during the trial experience we are asking:

1) "How do you feel so far Mrs. Robinson? Is this different from the way you would have tried it?"
2) "Could you see yourself getting some results if you were to do this consistently?"
3) "What do you think of our facility? Is it comfortable for you?"

When asked professionally, the responses to these sample questions will provide information about how receptive or comfortable the Prospect is at any point in the presentation. It might be in words, tonality or simply in body language, but the Prospect is always informing, in discrete and/or open ways how they are actually feeling. Ask questions and be aware of where the Prospect is in the buying process.

PRICING, PITCHING and ASKING FOR THE SALE

The time will come when it is necessary to finally disclose and discuss the price, and ask for the sale. That moment might be likened to asking for that first kiss. If everything has been prepared correctly and the mood has been set, all should go smoothly. Just as we know when it's the right time to ask with confidence for that first kiss, so we also know, with similar confidence, when is the correct moment to price and close the sale.

Statistically, experience suggests that there are, better chances of the Prospect making buying decisions when seated. So, after the presentation, and when you are confident you have aligned your ideas, product or service with the Prospect's needs, ask a couple more 'yes' questions to maintain the mood of optimism. "Do you like it here?", "Do you like the music?" "Did you like how things have been explained?" are all examples of 'yes' questions.

When closing, if there are 3 simple options, there is a high probability that the favoured choice will be the middle option. So, price and present the choices based on the idea of shooting for the stars, and hitting the moon.

Here is my suggested approach on the vital topic of pricing.

1) Offer a Premium Option that contains the most value. This option isn't for everyone. It is for the affluent. It is a premium service with the most extras and it is the most expensive ticket option that you offer.

2) The middle option offers excellent value at an afford-able price. This option is, and will be, the perfect fit. It maintains perfectly calculated margins and makes the most sense to everyone involved. This is the price around which a business model is built and that model will bring the majority of your sales.

3) This 3rd option will represent the least value with the highest price. This option is for the uncommitted 'punch card' Prospects, and in reality, is not the intended sale. The option is presented here for contrast, and to make the middle or Premium packages look even more appealing.

I have learned to always lead with the scariest price, then the middle option and finally the 3rd. This technique will always make the middle price (the target) seem more appealing and less intimidating. Shoot for the stars, hit the moon.

After describing all 3 options, it's time to ask for the sale. This can be done in so many ways. Questions such as "Which option works best for you?" or "Great - let's get you started!" - and start filling out the paper work – are reliable closes and work well. At this point the Prospect will either provide their critical, personal purchase information or raise further objections. If the presentation sales process has been performed correctly, it's 'pen to paper' time.

Overcoming Objections

Now, don't be disheartened if a point has been missed and an objection has been raised. Don't despair. This doesn't mean the deal is the dead. It simply means that there wasn't enough value created and some information wasn't clearly received by you or the Prospect. We now need to re-examine the steps and find what was missed.

Often an objection is disguised as "Can I think about it?" Don't be scared to find out what needs to be 'thought about'. Find out what additional information is needed to make the decision to proceed. Relax and talk about goals again. Go through the What, Why, When, Where and How to isolate where the resistance is. Maintain energy and remain confident, always certain of your product or service. Ask for the sale again with persistence and light heartedness. Like a best friend in the room, the seller becomes an assistant buyer and encourages our friend to take the purchase step.

In the words of **Rick Roberge, Sales Mentor**

"I believe in those professional salespeople who understand they are responsible for their prospect's comfort, needs, honesty, or lack thereof. It is the salesperson's job to discern if it's a fit. Not the other way around. It's the salesperson's duty to be the person that a buyer needs them to be, but not necessarily the person that the buyer wants them to be."

The Post Close

Be aware of 'Buyer's Remorse' but do not fear it. Doubt and hesitation are a natural part of the process. The key is to be prepared for it and prevent it as effectively as possible. There is a technique that can be used called the 'post close'. The 'post close' is like the cherry on top of a smooth transaction and will decrease the amount of potential cancellations.

After the sale has been made it is important and professional to ask a customer how they feel about the decision they have just made. Let the customer know that you are excited for them because they now have a road map, plan, strategy and solution to the problem that they came to solve.

Explain to the customer that they may experience a series of emotions about this investment. Explain that this is normal. A customer may find them self thinking more about the money instead of the outcome. Sometimes people in their life will try to talk them out of their decision. Remind of the very important promise, made at the outset, that this investment is properly and personally deserved. In expressing understanding that these emotions are possible, the customer is helped to cope with those feelings and a cancellation can be avoided.

The B-Back Bus

One of the most discouraging phrases that we hear, as sellers, is "I need to think about it. I will be back." After successfully determining a Prospect's WHAT, WHY, WHEN and HOW, still we hear the uncertainty expressed in the most discouraging of words - "I will be back". What now?

Statistically, the chances of that B-BACK bus pulling up are very low. Probably the deal is dead. In accepting this unfortunate probability, here is some perspective, based on thousands of presentations.

The test close is intended to help determine where the Prospect is in the buying process. We don't want to move to a close if the Prospect is not yet persuaded. Experience, intuition and questions will inform where the process stands. If the time comes to price or pitch and you are not convinced that the value has been conclusively communicated, delay the close. Book another time to visit and take a soft approach. This will work well if there has already been a disclosure that a spouse or other person may be involved in the decision-making process. In such a case, proceed to 'soft sell' with sincerity.

When it is possible to judge in advance that another visit will be needed, avoid pricing at this point and/or provide a low barrier offer to encourage the return visit.. Often, it is difficult for the Prospect to convey an accurate and effective message, the way you were able to, about value and detail, to their spouse or co-decider. This is what often leads to the 'hard no'. Your B-Back bus will likely not be pulling up.

Follow Up

This book clearly emphasizes how important it is to stay with a plan, step by step. One of the most important, yet often overlooked steps, is 'Follow-Up'. Be sure to 'Follow-Up' with everyone on everything.

When campaigning be sure to follow up every 3 days with all of the people who did not initially respond, and try again to book a visit. Try different words and try slightly different questions. The key here is to encourage, with sincerity, the initial personal action and step that will bring enhanced quality of life. Sometimes, people need a friendly reminder. Never be aggressive.

Every 'no-show' appointment also needs to be followed up. This is a process of rinse, wash and repeat. Be a professional and stay on top of appointments.

Every B-Back needs a follow up. Even if the chances are low that there will ultimately be a purchase, there is still a job to be done. Perhaps there are just one or two questions yet to be asked before the purchase can be finalized. Occasionally we can ask the prospect what could have been done better – what would have made a difference? Don't ask as an attempt to save the deal. Ask as a learning opportunity with the objective never again to make whatever mistake the Prospect identifies.

Projections

The concept of projecting an outcome is very important in the sales profession and examples can always be found in daily life.

Without a speedometer in a vehicle, we would be guessing speed and journey times. With access to the speedometer there can be an accurate prediction of journey times and outcomes.

This perspective needs to be applied to tracking sales results. At any current pace, when will $150,000 have been saved? What is the relevant daily sales average? It's common for tracking and projections to be delayed until the end of the month. With this type of untimely delay it's no wonder why targets and goals are missed.

Keep a finger on the pulse of the business by knowing the speed and pace at which things are happening or not happening. Be always conscious of projections and commitments. Use whatever analysis tools are comfortable – anything from Excel to white boards and wall calendars – but do track and constantly calculate performance

Who is a Client?

A Client is a customer who buys more than once. A Client is someone who has benefited from your ideas, product or service and continues to buy from you. We want to develop ongoing professional relationships with clients that always result in repeat business and predictable income. Remember - it always costs more to generate new customers than it does to keep existing clients. Focus on long-term service and you will have long-term clients. Keep your clients happy by keeping their needs met. Establish strategies, staff and systems that work to consistently maintain a high and predicable standard of service.

Who is a Community Member?

A broad customer base of Community Members will always be a priority goal. Such a base adds value for all who have a stake in any business.. When a Client trusts a business or sales professional enough to send referrals, we can define that Client as a Community Member. Helping grow the network of customer connections is what a Community Member can do. Community Members do this naturally because they are living and loving the ideas, service or product of the business. Community Members have been positively impacted and trust that the same experience can be available to friends and family.

Step 2 Review Questions

Take time to write down your answers to the following questions and put them somewhere that you will be reminded of them every day.

1) Who is a Suspect?
2) Who is a Prospect?
3) Who is a Customer?
4) Who is a Client?
5) Who is a Community Member?
6) How do you generate leads?
7) Who is your target market?
8) What are your top 3 lead sources?
9) What percentage of communication is with words?
10) What percentage of communication is through tonality?
11) What percentage of communication is conveyed with body language?
12) What are the 3 different pricing options?
13) What are 3 things that must apply for a Prospect to be considered qualified?

STEP 3
MAINTAIN THE 4 R'S

When enough Community Members are attracted and identified, we can see the amazing positive potential that comes with the opportunity to help many people. This cycle naturally gets replicated through renewals and referrals, becoming a vital business growth formula.

R #1 Results

Remember, whenever promised results are delivered, everybody wins.

In the fitness industry I have learned that Mrs. Robinson can be motivated, excited and encouraged by us at all times, but ultimately, if she doesn't achieve her goals, she will quit. Results take over as the primary motivation. If Mrs. Robinson feels that her goals are being achieved or exceeded, then she will become even more dedicated. It will be noticed that Mrs. Robinson is naturally eating better with every choice. She will be putting more thought into her food preparation, drinking more water, and generally following a healthier life regimen. This pattern prevails not because she was instructed, but because it is working for her.

Positive results lead to momentum. One of the best feelings in the world is gaining momentum toward achieving a goal. We all know that feeling. Knowing that we are growing in the right direction is one of the needs of the soul. That positive knowledge produces even more energy. It's a particularly gratifying feeling to experience the successful product of hard work and dedication.

Result oriented performance tracking is a very useful tool in setting realistic targets and remaining positively motivated.

By diligently tracking measurable performance results, opportunities are created to help so many more people.

In short, constant review of progress and results will inform whether or not the road map that was designed in Step 1 is being followed. Are the daily, weekly, monthly, quarterly and annual targets being met? Are the sales campaigns and strategies succeeding?

KNOW WHAT IS WORKING and KNOW WHAT IS NOT.

We can all recall being taught that a definition of insanity is doing the same thing over-and-over again and expecting a different result each time.

I recently researched this popular aphorism and found it's not really true, so I am not going to recommend it as a formula to live by. However I will agree that repeating the same unsuccessful methods and tasks can be frustrating and a terrible waste of energy.

In the world of sales & marketing, however, there is a degree of repetition and rejection that must be accepted and handled. I quickly learned that a measurable percentage of people will always say "no", regardless of the proposition presented to them. I learned to accept this fact, entirely, and move ahead to more productive opportunities. The secret was to track how many "no's" lead to a "yes" because enough "no's" ALWAYS lead to the eventual "yes".

R #2 Ratios

In sales we are very much in a numbers game. Accordingly it's essential to monitor and maintain consciousness of success ratios. That means tracking everything and avoiding 'winging it'. Simply tracking performance can have the effect of naturally improving performance.

Maybe I have an instinctive drive to outperform myself, or the magical power of concentrated focus, but where my attention goes, so does my energy.

In my career I've been able to rapidly increase my productivity by always analyzing exactly how we are performing. It's the only way to see and promote improvement in performance. By accurately being able to predict our performance, we can determine where to put resources and scale strategies, accordingly. This is very much about knowing strengths and weaknesses.

Here are some of the important ratios that should always be tracked.

- **CONTACTED**

How many leads were created in a campaign and how many resulted in a positive connection? Making quality connections is the purpose of a successful campaign. Do not put the pressure on a campaign to close deals. A quality close will happen later and naturally, depending on how well the connection is tracked and how well the process follows the professional steps.

So, first, focus on lead generation when campaigning and then be diligent with tracking those leads. It is important to know this so that the effectiveness and successful direction of marketing dollars can be analyzed and effectively directed in future campaigns. Wasting resources on unsuccessful campaigns is the fastest way to go out of business. For example, frequently 80% of leads come from 20% of lead sources. If attention is not paid to this, many quality opportunities can be missed. Focus more resources on the 20% that produce the most results and magic happens!

- **BOOKED**

Here are more tracking questions. Ask yourself - How many contacts did I book? How many out of 20 contacts am I booking? What is the percentage? Be honest and be consistent with this because this will determine the success of future efforts and marketing investments, moving forward. 70% -90% booking ratios are very attainable when using 'gated questioning'.

One of the best pieces of advice I recall receiving when considering booking techniques, was to 'sell the sizzle, not the steak'. This means, when booking, we are trying to resonate with needs and desires. Before committing to further action there is a hunger to know more. For the Prospect to be encouraged to take further action we need to stay sharp. Energy, enthusiasm and sincerity will maintain a Prospect's interest. Wanting more and following the scent of sweet sizzle will certainly lead the hungry Prospect to the idea, service or product.

Imagine asking someone out on a date. Prior to a first dinner or hang out, would it be most effective to immediately explain the full detail of your dating history, sexual fantasies, life goals and family history, all in the initial invitation conversation? To be honest, I have tried that approach, and although I did get some results, the ratios were low. I do not recommend it.

▪ SHOWED/NO SHOWED

How many booked appointments are showing up and are moved to the presentation step? It is so important to be aware of this statistic. It is possible to experience the frustration of a full day of booked appointments turning into a day of NO-SHOWS. No business and no sales - nothing can be salvaged on those days. What to do? Confirmed appointments will always increase show ratios. Be diligent and follow professional steps to ensure that Prospects attend the appointments, as arranged.

▪ CLOSED

How many Prospects are being converted into Customers? 80-90% is a very possible when following the steps of qualifying, questioning and creating value. Remember, - 'closing' is a formula and technique that can be learned and mastered. Once the techniques of 'closing' are mastered, the simple task becomes one of maximizing the numbers of Prospects attracted to attend appointments.

- **B-BACKS**

How many prospects who promise to return actually do return? I have seen the softest of sellers maintain highest positive B-Back ratios. A benefit of the soft sell is that that the Prospect still likes you and feels comfortable enough to come back. I'll share, here, the uncomfortable fact that there have been times in my career when I pushed too hard. My prospects did not come back. In fact, at one point I was known for averaging 10% B-back because I burned many bridges by hard selling. So be warned! Elegance is the key and always worth striving for.

R #3 Renewals & Repeat Business

Creating repeat business with consistency is a desired, end-result. A business that is sustained, substantially, by Clients and Community Members that are constantly enhancing the quality of their lives, is a model of sustainability. A mutual relationship built on the principals of 'give and take' between you and your community is a necessary and worthy objective..

Low renewal ratios can be likened to houses built quick-sand. It's not possible to frame or build walls because the building is always sinking. If Customer and Client renewals are low and people aren't coming back more than once, the business might be built on quick- sand. In these situations re-evaluate how the Client is being served and look more closely at the situation from the perspective of the Client rather than your own. In other words – employ empathy. Renewals are the sign of a healthy business. Non-Renewals may be the sign of an unsustainable business.

Tracking RENEWAL RATIOS is a crucial step to determining business sustainability. Build a data base of renewing business by knowing where the leaks are. How many Customers are staying? How many Customers are leaving? Why are they leaving? What is it costing every time a Customer is lost? What is it costing every time a Customer is gained? What does it cost to retain a Client?

When I was 14 years old I met a very inspiring man named Jeff. Jeff was so cool and really resonated with me. The way this man carried himself was so smooth and charismatic. He seemed to never have a stress in the world and seemed to move at his own pace. He was in his mid 40's and trained in martial arts. He would come in and do private lessons at mid-day with our head instructor and then come back again in the evening.

One day I asked him, "Jeff, how come you are able to come here twice a day? I know you have two young daughters and most people I know with kids, are working a lot and barely have time for training. You never seem rushed and are always able to focus when training. What is your secret?"

Jeff answered my question with two words, "Predictable Income", and then drove away in his new car. I had to know more, so the next time I saw Jeff I cornered him. I squeezed him for more information and he explained to me that his family business was a dance academy. They had 350 members who all attended classes and paid a monthly fee. Over years the business had built such a loyal following that eventually his family had no shortage of time, health and money.

That was a 'light bulb over my head' moment. I remember having to do an assignment the following week in school about our futures. 'Predicable Income' was very much my theme and target.

Remember to ALWAYS renew your # 1 Client - YOU! Being able to consistently renew energy and spirit by reflecting on, and recalling, vision, purpose and passion, always brings healthy Renewal. Be the 'constant' in your own life and always stay renewed on your quest and goals. Never forget your targets, checkpoints and projections. Find ways to keep yourself fresh and motivated. Visualizations, mantras, audio programs, books, and masterminding with other motivated people, are all effective ways to maintain healthy renewal.

3 Tips to Increase Renewals

1) Succeed with the promised results and then exceed those results.
2) Build a friendly but professional relationship. Friends buy from friends.
3) Be dependable, consistent and reliable because stability and loyalty always succeed.

4 Referrals

We know that we are producing results when a Client trusts enough to refer their friends, family or co-workers. When such a positive impact has been made that a Client is encouraging others to also benefit from your ideas, service or product, is when the Referral Zone has been entered This is the zone that will enable contributions to the world on a measurable level, particularly through the power of social networks.

A business grows with the magical compounding effect of producing results, good ratios, renewals and referrals. Consider the potential effect that one happy Community Member can have on a business. That Member can send a friend, who sends a friend, who sends another friend, who sends a friend - and so on. This Customer, who was once only a Suspect, eventually can convert tens - even hundreds - of happy, new, COMMUNITY MEMBERS.

The power of 'word of mouth' can be your best friend or your worst enemy. If follow-through with service is inadequate and not getting expected results, referrals will not happen. In fact the potential damage does not stop there. If Mrs. Robinson does not get what you promised, she will refer her network in the opposite direction. As Grant Cardone says, "our network is our net-worth and it is amazing to see how fast things can spread about you or your service, now, with social media."

I remember working with a guy at a fitness business in Ontario in 2002. This guy wasn't much for phone work or setting up many appointments. He would have 1/3 of the appointments in the book each day, as I would, but would always close the day with lots of deals. His secret? He was a referral machine. Always at unexpected times a Community Member would walk a friend, family or co-worker straight into his pocket. It was so predicable - almost like clock-work, and made very clear the power of business referrals.

According to Geoffrey James, contributing editor at inc.com, here are 3 Tips to remember when asking for referrals.

3 Tips for Asking for Referalls

1) Ask After Delivery, Not After Closing.
"Many sales pros make the huge mistake of asking for a referral right after they've closed the deal. That's dumb, because you've just asked the customer to take a risk by buying from you. Why would the customer want to take another risk and refer a colleague to you? Therefore, rather than asking for the referral outright, ask for the "right to ask." Here's how.

When the customer says "yes", say something like:

Wonderful! Thanks for agreeing to become our customer. I have one request. I want you to think of some friends and colleagues who you think should be doing business with us — providing we are as incredible as I've been claiming we are. Once I have proven to you, beyond all doubt, that we can deliver and delight you, I'm going ask you to contact those people to suggest they meet with me. Does that sound fair?"

Then follow up... after you're certain that you've wowed the customer. Note: this tactic comes from a conversation with uber-guru Jeffrey Gitomer, author of classic book: The Sales Bible."

2) Give Your Customer a Referral First.

"This one is so simple that it's crazy that more sales pros don't use it. Because you're in sales, you know lots of people, right? If you use those connections to bring in some extra business for your Prospect, you've earned the right – tit for tat – to ask for a referral.

The great thing about this idea is that it really does put you into the proverbial "win-win" scenario. More money coming into your customer, means that they'll have more money to spend - capeesh? Note: I originally heard this tactic from Sam Reese, CEO of the huge sales training firm Miller Heiman."

3) Have Your Customer Contact the Prospect.

"Once you get an agreement for your customer to give you a referral, don't settle for contact information. While you can always say something like "Joe told me to contact you," such phrases are used so frequently that they're meaningless. For all the contact knows, Joe might have given you his name simply to get rid of you! (Don't laugh; happens all the time.)

Instead, get your colleague to take a specific action that brings you together with the Prospect. Rather than asking for a name and number, ask the referrer to call and explain who you are and why you are worth having a conversation with. Ask the referrer to get back to you to confirm that the call has been made or send an email (and copy you on the email).

Then follow up!"

Note: This tactic comes from a conversation with one of my favorite people: Joanne Black, author of the extremely useful book No More Cold Calling."

It is very important to maintain incredible service and get your promised results. Renew your Clients and become part of their network, always marketing your ideas, services and products. Marketing messages that change the world from the inside out are quickly contagious – in a good way!. Infect the world with your passion, your certainty and your influence. Make a positive and passionate impact in people's lives.

Step 3 Review Questions

Take time to write down your answers to the following questions.

1) What results do you promise to produce with your idea, service or product?
2) What are your booking ratios?
3) What are your show ratios?
4) What are your closing ratios?
5) What are your B-Back ratios?
6) What are your renewal ratios?
7) How many referrals did you get last month?
8) What are your sales projections this month?

ADDITIONAL CONTENT FOR ADDED VALUE

Congratulations and thank you for making it this far in the program. Since you are still with me, then it might be safe to say that we are heading in the right direction and you are feeling the message. This next chapter contains additional information that can be useful in streamlining results. I wish someone had informed me of this content earlier in my career!

Delegating

If you are an entrepreneur, team leader, parent or even a band member, it is important to understand the power of delegation. Finding the right person for the best performance is key. Every individual has strengths and weaknesses. As a collective, a group of individuals can balance each other out.

"The person in the room who thinks they know the most, in fact, likely knows the least." That statement reminds me that there are always people better skilled than I am in many areas and tasks. It is ok and constructive to harness the power of another's skill-set to help achieve a goal. Focus on your own skill set and be ready to add it to the mix when the time comes.

A true leader can identify a person's gifts and encourage them to their full potential. Getting out of the way is the art of a leader. Showing a team what top performance looks like will enable that team to shine. When duties and responsibilities are successfully delegated to the most appropriate people, there will be a significant impact on the ability to focus on sales and marketing. Believe in your people.

Raise Your Standards

I feel very passionate about this topic because it is probably the most important issue in resolving one's inner conflict.

Our standards determine our outcome. When, in my previous life, I unwisely associated myself with drug abusers, I felt like a boss. It was easy to match or beat the standards with which I surrounded myself.

It wasn't until I started to associate with self-made millionaires that I noticed a difference in the way that they looked at the world and the standards that they set. So, adopt the perspectives of the people you want to be like and don't settle for less.

I have learned that just because a particular individual has been around for a long time doesn't mean they should continue to be. Please don't misunderstand me. I very much believe in loyalty. However, if you are not inspired, motivated or encouraged by someone in your life, and you begin to feel as if you are on separate paths, it is ok to consider altering the nature of your association with them from friendship to acquaintanceship.

Reposition them in your inner circle so that your standards remain high. Expect more from the people around you and you will expect more from yourself.

How to Fix Bad Credit

When it comes to credit, there is no way around it. I abused every single resource available to me in my attempts to build credit. The 'easy to obtain' student loans and entry level credit cards were all maxed, with no payments. In fact, I spent my entire student loan money on non-school related spending and never properly attended college. Needless to say, I dropped out of college with nothing but debt. Since I never made a single payment on my credit cards, student loans or taxes, the tax authorities froze my accounts and flexed their muscle.

7 Steps to Fixing Bad Credit

1) Save the most that you can afford each month, after essential spending. If you want to fix the mess, save some money.

2) Take your money to a bank that allows pre-paid credit cards and buy one. $250 -$500 will do it.

3) Use this card like a normal credit card and a responsible person. Buy a couple of items with the card and then pay back immediately. This is the important part. Don't repeat the mistakes that created the mess in the first place. Use the credit card and pay its balance, reliably. This will start to build trust again between you and the bank.

4) After doing this for 12-18 months, go to the bank and ask them to remove the hold. That means returning to you the $250-$500 you pre-paid. If you did step 3 correctly, the bank will allow this. You will now have a low credit score but at least you have a score again.

5) After 6 months of using your low limit credit card consistently and responsibly, you can ask the bank for small available credit increase. You'll be moving up in the world.

6) Now, use your new minimal credit score to get a phone. You now have the chance to have another company vouch for you with the credit reporting bureau. Pay your phone bill automatically so that you don't miss your payments.

7) Lease a car. Depending on interest rates of course, you will have a better chance of leasing rather than buying. Leasing a car is not unlike renting a car, and the car company may feel it has more control over your performance in the deal.

Using these 3 sources of credit (credit card, phone and vehicle lease) consistently and responsibly, your credit score will recover. These 7 steps will take 2-3 years but will be worth the effort. Learn from the mistakes and do not repeat them. Good credit will be needed to buy real estate, borrow money, lease spaces, and eventually to provide for your family. The feeling of a second chance is a great one. It's vital not to abuse it.

Find a Mentor

For me, growing up without a consistent, guiding parental figure had a significant negative impact on my psyche. Unable to clearly decide which choices were correct, I experimented with many different approaches. Some were effective and others were not.

As a young martial artist I discovered the difference having a Sensei could make in a boy's life. He was someone who would teach, demonstrate, persuade and influence me in the right direction. That was the role of my Sensei. My Sensei could prevent me from repeating the same mistakes and perpetuating a downward spiral of self-defeat.

When it comes to Professional Sales, find someone who has mastered the necessary techniques and absorb as much information as possible. Copy the successful patterns and styles. Find a map, tool or a mentor who makes sense to you and do not try to reinvent the wheel. Listen to what you are told and study the successful actions and techniques.

If you do not know anybody who has attained the heights you want to attain, go to the internet. The range of resources available is amazing. Initially I consumed all of the free audio books that I could find on YouTube. It is incredible what people have provided for those who are willing to search and consume.

5 Things to Look for in a Great Mentor

1) Accountability. A great mentor is there for you every step of the way. In understanding you, a good mentor will keep you on track.

2) Clarity of purpose. A great mentor will help you understand your own needs and help you clearly define your path.

3) Education. A great mentor will take time to teach you the necessary steps, ensuring your best performance by preparing you properly.

4) Reliability. A great mentor is there for you whenever he/she is needed. You can count on your mentor to adapt and work with you during the ups and the downs.

5) Walk the walk. A great mentor has accomplished what you want to accomplish. Such a person does not just talk the talk. They have already taken the steps you need to take.

Tony Robbin's List of 6 Human Needs

I have quoted Tony Robbins many times in this book. That is because Tony has accomplished so much. I am truly inspired by everything that he does and his ability to give back to the world on such a significant and effective level.

Listening to Tony was the first time I heard this list. He may have created it himself or learned it from one of his teachers. One day I hope to have the opportunity to meet Tony and ask him about the original sources for his inspiration.

These 6 suggested ingredients, when balanced harmoniously, will provide a feeling of fulfillment. Find your perfect balance and discover how it makes sense in your life.

Here is Tony Robbins' list of our 6 NEEDS/DRIVES. Read them and ask if you are satisfying these needs within your own life. I found this strategy so useful. It deserved its own page.

1) **CERTAINTY** - We all have a need for stability, certainty and comfort.
2) **UNCERTAINTY/VARIETY**– We need to mix it up to prevent getting stale.
   "Without order, nothing exists. Without chaos, nothing evolves."
3) **TO FEEL LOVE/CONNECTION**– Love and cherish the relationships in our lives.
4) **TO FEEL SIGNFICANT**– We need to feel a purpose and a sense of importance.
   Next are the "needs of the SPIRIT".
5) TO GROW – Energy in motion must stay in motion - always evolving.
6) TO CONTRUBUTE BEYOND OURSELVES – We are a part of the collective and the illusion of the individual is short-sighted. Dissolve the ego and give back.

This list is written in plain sight - displayed in multiple places in my home. With honest reflection, I identify with my need for certainty. This is a reflection and result of my unsettled experiences as I was growing up. I also recognized my drive to feel significant, noticing myself seeking attention in social situations. Contributing beyond myself was very difficult. I had trained myself to always look out for # 1. In starting the Westcore Kids program, and opening the doors, free of charge, to the families that couldn't afford it, I suddenly felt that part of my heart for the first time.

I urge you, and anyone suffering, to go through this list and subject yourself to an honest review. We are all out of balance in one way or another. There is no static state of happiness. Identify, recognize and honor all the different depths and dimensions that make up your beautiful soul. Imagine a DJ perfectly matching the beat to multiple tracks in the same key. The DJ adds layers of beauty, making a unique experience of sound. This is your life and these are the tools. Build your own version of 'awesome' and play your song loudly.

Attitude of Gratitude

Be thankful for the blessings in your life. Everyone has someone or something to be thankful for.

If we were meeting, 1 on 1 I'd express this thought to you more clearly than can be found in the average 'business book'

"I mean really, fucken grateful for that shit, because if they weren't around, or if you didn't have it anymore, you would be a wreck."

I hope these words, if no others, ring forever in your ears.

We must always be grateful for our Health, Freedom, and Love. The heart and spirit will stay open and calm when you remind yourself, daily, of the things that you are grateful for.

Fear, insecurities, doubts, anxieties and even attachment, all start to dissolve when you are in a state of gratitude. Gratitude is a tool and strategy that sounds vague at this time, but will help you sleep at night when life gets complicated and overwhelming.

Remember what you are grateful for and remind yourself, every day, to savor the warm feeling of a thankful heart. Life itself is a blessing, and you are a miracle.

I am reminded of an elderly man named John I once knew, when I think of gratitude. John was a neat old dude who I would see every night at the local hotel hot tub, which I would often visit. John and I would talk about random things while relaxing in the warm water. He told stories of his time during World War 2, and of the violence and suffering he had witnessed. He lost 3 of his closest friends in that war. It was a terrible time for him.

John raised 3 children with his wife Helen. Helen had passed 5 years previously and it was a difficult time for everyone who loved her. One of John's children had died in a car crash at age 21. John had experienced terrible times.

One day, while talking with John, I had a very emotional moment. I had asked him, with my whole heart, and sincerity, "John, having been through so much pain and suffering, how do you still smile? How are you so engaging of everyone around you and not defeated like most people might be?"

John replied. "Well, young fella, I've learned that it's all about where I am looking. I can stare backwards, being paralyzed by pain, or I can look forward and be grateful for all of the beauty. I am grateful every-day that I wake up on this side of the dirt, because it is another chance to make a great memory for myself or someone else."

I will never forget this conversation with John. When I am overwhelmed or attached to a present moment of stress, I try to think of John and be grateful that I am on this side of the dirt, making positive memories for myself or someone else.

The Power of Taking-Action

After understanding and internalizing the different ideas, energies and common themes of the great people who inspire me, I have learned, at the end of the day, that success and effectiveness can always be found in the person who takes the most action. Potential and success is not about the most educated. Whoever is willing to commit themselves to a plan and is prepared to get dirty, is the one who will taste success. Paralysis of analysis is a real state of mind. It is easy to just listen, read, watch videos and theorize. Taking the first steps to actualize the theories is not so easy. It can be uncomfortable and unnatural. Remember, though, repetition gives birth to skill.

The universe likes action and I can tell you that once you start to put your plan into action, you will soon and inevitably see results. Commit to action, you will experience the momentum of success. Whatever your goal may be, step out of your comfort zone and take the steps that you wrote down in Step 1. Your clear and logical plan requires your commitment and dedication.

I know a guy who has advanced university degrees and has read uncounted books. He's read books on sales, business, development, etc. - this guy has read them all. Although he is a very interesting person to talk to, he hasn't made any measurable strides in his life in the past 5 years that I have known him. It is puzzling because he knows so much more than I do, academically, but hasn't acted, in practical terms, on that academic advantage.. This is what I call the 'know-it-all' phenomena. I have learned that we must also become a 'do-it-all' person. Stop only thinking and start doing.

For example, for me, the thought of writing this book was a very scary and daunting idea. I knew that I had accumulated enough knowledge and experience to share, but was my message relevant? Was it worth taking the time to write a step-by-step guide on how to sell?

I can say that, after writing this book, I feel more confident than ever in my own ability to convey and teach these messages. I am proud of my work and can confidently say that I have now written my first book. I acted on an idea. I took action. That is the key. Giving back to the world and hopefully assisting anyone who reads it.

Each time I look back at the periods in my life that were the hardest and most stressful, I am reminded of the action steps that I took that were triggered by unsustainable and unacceptable discomfort. My suggestion is to not wait for situations to become too painful, as I did. Make the changes now, focusing on the comfort of your potential accomplishments, and let that excitement be your motivation.

On the topic of taking-action, I am reminded Gary Vaynerchuk. Gary has passion, purpose and drive. He is the author of the book 'Crush It'. Gary embodies the term 'hustle', and lives his life in one big momentum of action and results. A self-made millionaire who is 'self-driven', Gary really takes the term 'Massive Action', to an entirely new level. With this in mind, here is one of my favorite Gary V quotes.

> "All your ideas may be solid or even good, but you have to actually EXECUTE on them for them to matter." – *Gary Vaynerchuk*

Make people your passion and you will find your purpose. Influence, inspire, motivate, teach, learn, and sell. Sell with your whole heart and help others find their WHAT, WHY, WHEN and "HOW?" This is what will perpetuate life and inspire greatness. Don't sell for the money or the power. Persuade and sell to make a difference in the world and you will see how that power multiplies 10X its value in your own life as well.

Engage people. Wake them up and light a fire within them. Everybody needs value in their lives and everybody needs help developing that value. If you have an idea, service or product that will enhance the quality of people's lives, sell it, and sell it proudly.

Directly enhancing the quality of life with ideas, values, thoughts, services and products is your duty as a thought leader, parent, influencer, persuader or seller. Be consistent with your focus, systems and values but do remember - Sell Yourself First.

Suggested Reads

1) "Rich Dad, Poor Dad" Robert Kiyosaki
2) "The 10x RULE" Grant Cardone
3) "As a Man Thinketh" James Allen
4) "Secrets of Closing the Sale" Zig Ziglar
5) "Power of Influence" Anthony Robbins
6) "7 Habits of Highly Effective People" Stephen R. Covey
7) "If you're not first, you're last" Grant Cardone
8) "Think and Grow Rich" Napolean Hill
9) "How to win friends and Influence People" Dale Carnegie
10) "Psycho Cybernetics" Maxwell Maltz
11) "To sell is human" Daniel Pink
12) "Power vs Force" Dr. David Hawkins
13) "Unlimited Power" Anthony Robbins
14) "The BIG Leap" Gay Hendricks
15) "The little Book of Trading" Michael Covel

ABOUT THE AUTHOR

Mike is a Drummer, Kumo Jiu Jitsu Black Belt, Successful Entrepreneur and Author. Devoted to growth, Mike has been selling his entire life with passion and intensity. A self-admitted f*ck up, he knows all too well what it is like to dig himself into a hole and climb out.

Having experienced more than his share of pain and suffering as a youth, Mike experimented with many unwise experiences. Never wanting to 'follow suit', he challenged authority and himself, taking everything to the extreme. In his late teens and early twenties, Mike behaved criminally. From selling and abusing drugs to engaging in activities best not mentioned, his actions led to multiple arrests and a lengthy criminal record.

When Mike discovered the power of commission sales, he found hope. By learning to sell fitness and martial arts memberships, Mike carved out a niche and finally established his path. Settling into Victoria BC, Mike has set sales records at every company he has ever sold for. Implementing systems as a contracted salesperson at many small fitness businesses was something that came easy and early for Mike. By 25 years old, Mike had successfully opened or helped open multiple private fitness studios.

A decade later, at age 35, Mike now owns and operates Westcore Training Centre. Westcore is a successful Fitness and Martial Arts company that directly enhances the quality of hundreds of lives every week. He is actively growing and sustaining an annual multiple 6 figure investment portfolio that consists of businesses, real estate rental units and stocks.

Mike has learned the power of being focused and resourceful. He now enjoys measurable successes in his life and is dedicated to contributing to society and the world on a massive level. Spending time daily with his Westcore Kids program is a passion for Mike. This is the opportunity for Mike to teach the skills passed to him by his first Sensei/Mentor, Darrell LaFrance.

Darrell was the first adult to believe in Mike and empowered him with the skills to survive. He taught Mike Japanese Jiu Jitsu, Brazilian Jiu Jitsu, Judo, Karate, culminating in awarding Mike his Black Belt in Kumo Jiu Jitsu. This was a very a proud and pivotal moment for Mike.

With discipline and focus, Mike has chosen to be a force for good in a world of confusion. Mike remains entirely committed to helping others learn the same tools, strategies and techniques that helped him 'unf*ck' himself.

———

52530852R00060

Made in the USA
San Bernardino, CA
23 August 2017